APRICOTS
AND
TORTILLAS

APRICOTS
AND
TORTILLAS

An Anthology about Growing Up
in Albuquerque
in the Postwar Years

SUSAN PAQUET, EDITOR

Apricots and Tortillas:
An Anthology about Growing Up
in Albuquerque in the Postwar Years
Copyright ©2015 Susan Paquet
ISBN: 978-1-940769-35-6

Publisher: Mercury HeartLink

Requests for permission to make copies of this work,
or inquiries about presentations may be sent to:
susan@susanpaquet.com.

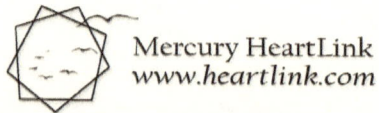

Mercury HeartLink
www.heartlink.com

Apricots and Tortillas

Introduction

The Stories

Susan Paquet

Lisa Myers

Maria Leyba

Author Biographies

Introduction

In this nostalgic rendition of postwar Albuquerque in the Fifties and Sixties, seven authors bring their unique perspectives as they share memories of growing up in what could be described as a "Norman Rockwell" time in our country's history.

Albuquerque, nestled in the "Land of Enchantment," is one of New Mexico's special treasures. It is known for its rich beauty, with the Sandia Mountains spreading watermelon hues at sunset, its endless days of sunshine and blue skies inspiring artists from all over the world, and its cultural diversity which weaves Native, Hispanic, African-American, Asian, and Caucasian cultures together while still allowing each to have its own individuality. To the east are the "faldas," the skirts of the Sandia Mountains; to the north and south are the Native pueblos; to the west are the vast desert mesas. All are nurtured and sustained by the life-giving waters of the Rio Grande.

This anthology features seven authors from various ethnic and cultural backgrounds who tell their stories of childhood. No two stories are the same. One takes you to the candy counter at Fedway Department Store. Another talks about the debilitating disease of polio. Some stories hint at discrimination and cruelty, a reality during that time in history. One story deals with the devastation of the Bataan Death March from a child's point of view. One deals with the Fourth of July, not as a patriotic holiday, but as an adventure into the vast world of fireworks.

These stories will move you to laughter and to tears. More importantly, you will share the optimism of our writers and the nostalgia of the times as you are reminded of the taste of fresh apricot empanadas, the aroma of warm buttered tortillas, the sweet honey combined with puffy sopapillas, and the magic that was once childhood in Albuquerque, New Mexico.

THE STORIES

Susan Paquet

Naming Me Nieves

It was my first day of school and I was excited. It was 1952 and I was beginning first grade at Emerson Elementary School in Albuquerque, New Mexico. I skipped out of my house carrying a Cinderella lunch box and thermos in my hand. I could hardly wait to get to school and learn how to read.

No sooner had I sat down at my desk than I realized school was not what I had expected. I had a big problem. I was six years old and for the first time understood what it meant not to belong. Children in my school were Hispanic, American Indian, or Military. I was none of the above, and I was worried.

School personnel from the main office had come to our classroom to count us based on federal funding available for certain categories of students. The American Indian children were asked come to the front of the classroom. The office personnel zealously counted said children and funds from the Bureau of Indian Affairs. Next the Military children were asked to come to the front of the classroom. The office personnel zealously counted said children and funds from the Department of Defense. Federal funding was not available during this era for Hispanic students or "the other," meaning myself.

I was left sitting with the Hispanic students. They were

all beautiful children who had bright brown eyes, thick dark hair and skin the color of cinnamon spice. I looked all wrong. Granted, my eyes were brown, and my hair was dark. However, my hair hung from a limp ponytail in thin strands, not the rich, thick, flowing hair of the other seated children. My hair situation was problem enough, but my skin color was a disaster. It was not the rich flavor of spice; it was the white of paste. I was not Hispanic. I looked like the Military children, but my father was a mere civilian in the plumbing business.

Where was a little girl with limp hair, skin the color of paste and a father in the plumbing business going to belong?

I quickly decided that I was a Military and went to the front of the classroom. The school personnel eagerly counted me without question.

The problem did not come until several days later. Thinking my secret was safe, I actually began to see myself as a Military. I decided to elaborate on my identity when I played with the kids. I told tales about my family being recently stationed in Guam. I had no idea where or what Guam might be, no idea it was an ocean island. I just knew many of the Militaries had lived on Guam. A couple of days later we were talking about seashells, beaches, and oceans. I said I had never seen an ocean. At that point little Jenny, know-it-all (there is one in every group), said, "But you lived in Guam." Jenny put her hands on her hips and smirked, "Guam is an island, an island on the ocean." My house of cards began to fall. I decided to pull rank on her as I had seen the other Militaries do. I screamed, "My father will tell you we lived in Guam, he is an Admiral in the Army." The other kids grew silent, and then began to laugh. They might have not yet learned to read and write, but a Military is taught from infancy their father's rank and branch of service. The Army has generals. Only the Navy has admirals. My house of cards, along with my temporary sense of identity, had been crushed.

I decided I would go back with the kids who had originally remained seated with me. I knew I was not Hispanic, but was fascinated by them. Actually, it was their language that fascinated me. It was so powerful and magical that they were forbidden to speak it in the classroom. If the teacher heard them speak Spanish they were sent to the principal's office to be paddled. I was often sent to the principal's office for paddling but for less interesting reasons such as leaving my desk without permission.

The teacher succeeded in forcing the Hispanic kids to stop speaking Spanish in the classroom, but what happens at recess stays at recess. Hidden behind the building they laughed and joked, eating piñon nuts and speaking Spanish. Their language was not harsh and choppy like English. Their language flowed softly, as if it were a mountain spring. I wanted the magic, the fresh mountain spring. The problem was the Hispanic kids did not want me.

I would sit on the gravel playground off to the side of their group, hoping to be included. I did this for a couple of weeks until accidentally I found my "inclusion" ticket. My mother always packed me a snack for recess. Usually it was something plain like graham crackers. One day she packed me not one but two Hostess Twinkies. The soft sponge cake with creamy filling made sitting in the gravel, alone, almost bearable.

One of the girls in the Hispanic group sat in front of me in the classroom. Her real name was Marisela, but the teacher had changed her name for the classroom to be Sally. The no Spanish rule applied even to names given to you by your parents at Baptism. I always thought the teacher had specifically chosen the name Sally because the teacher did not like Marisela. Sally was a terrible name and Marisela deserved better. Sally was the blond, curly, extremely boring girl in our reading book. Sally was the same girl who hung out with the equally boring Dick and Jane. Marisela was nothing like Sally. Marisela was fun, intelligent and independent.

Mariselsa and I talked frequently in the classroom, not only because we enjoyed each other's company, but because it irritated the teacher, who disliked me as well. The reason she disliked me had nothing to do with Marisela. It had to do with me being as the teacher described, "a stubborn, bull headed and willful child."

Anyway, the day I was eating the Hostess Twinkies,

Marisela came over to me and asked what I was eating. I told her a Hostess Twinkie and gave her one. She asked if she could also have the one I was eating. I gave them both to her. She took them over to the group and distributed them like the piñon nuts. I was in!

The girls decided that I needed a makeover, beginning with my skin. One of the girls snuck some of her mother's make-up to school. We all hoped it would give my white skin some color. It did indeed give me color, the dark of the make-up and the white of my skin blended into an awful color of orange. They tried to sun me, hoping for a cinnamon tan. I burned to the shade of red paprika. They gave up.

They had better luck with my hair, taking the thin, stringy strands and braiding them with ribbons. I was afraid my mother would not fix it that way for me, but even she admitted it was a solution for hair that was too thin and stringy even for an Anglo girl.

Marisela and I became best friends. Frequently we would go to each other's houses after school to play. Sometimes Marisela's mother, Mrs. Garcia, would invite me to stay for dinner. I was always glad to be included in the meal. Just being in Marisela's house made me hungry. The kitchen was a festival of colors and smells, as chile, onion, oregano, garlic and tortillas melted together into delicious enchiladas.

One time after dinner it started to snow. Not unheard of, but unusual for Albuquerque. Mrs. Garcia dialed my mother on the phone and asked if I could spend the night because of the weather. The next morning we woke up to houses, trees, yards and streets all covered with beautiful untouched snow. Mrs. Garcia started to cry, saying it made her homesick for her childhood in Northern New Mexico. Then Mrs. Garcia smiled at me. She said in her hometown a child born to the first snow of winter is always named Nieves. She told me it is a beautiful name and means snow in Spanish. She gently touched my white face and named me Nieves.

The teacher still insisted on calling me Susan in the classroom. But at recess I was Nieves, playing, laughing and eating piñon nuts with Marisela, Celestina, José, Miguel and the rest of the group.

Saint Valentine Day's Tragedy

It was second grade; it was Valentine's Day and all the kids were having a grand time. We had each decorated a shoebox with red construction-paper hearts and our names. Our parents had bought us inexpensive valentines that we put in everyone's box. The rules were clear. Everyone received a valentine from everyone, there were to be no hurt feelings. In addition, all of the parents purchased a nice valentine card for us to give to our teacher. Everyone gave the teacher a store-bought card, except for a Pueblo Indian boy named Otis.

To this day, it makes me sad. I liked Otis and the other Native American children. Even as a child I found their culture beautiful. My parents would take me to the nearby Indian Pueblos to watch the feast day dancing. The drum beat of the singing matched the beat of a God given heart. My parents would let me get fresh baked bread that came from round ovens known as *hornos*. The woman who baked the bread was like the grandmother of all grandmothers. She always bent down and smiled at me as if I were her own grandchild. She handed me the gift of bread as priest hands a communion wafer to a parishioner.

Otis had recently moved from the Pueblo to the city with his parents. He understood the drum beat of his Pueblo's heart, the Grandmother who gave the gift of bread on feast days. He did not understand store-bought valentine cards for the teacher. But Otis understood that Valentine's Day was a special day and the teacher was to be treated with respect. Otis gave the teacher his special gift, a loaf of bread. It was store bought, having no *horno* ovens in the city. I even remember the brand. It was Rainbow Bread.

The teacher laughed at him, made fun of him in front of the entire class. Otis did not cry but he put his head down and looked at his shoes. He kept his head down the rest of the school year.

Up until that day Valentine's Day had always been one of my favorite holidays. It was fun exchanging cards at school. Then when my father came home he would always bring my mother roses and me a box of candy. He didn't just give me the box of candy. He made me close my eyes and then hid the candy box, somehow combining the excitement of an Easter egg hunt and Valentine's Day into one. That night I didn't want to look for the candy. I ran to my room and burst into tears. My father was flabbergasted. I told him what had happened to Otis at school. My father hugged me and said he would take care of it.

Parents in those days never questioned the school's authority, but the next day my father went to the principal's office to complain about the teacher's treatment of Otis. Nothing changed at school. But I remember what my Dad did, forever, knowing valentines are much more than paper cards.

Malpais – "The Bad Lands"

The first day of third grade a volcano erupted in my classroom—not one of those modern day science projects of papier-mâché and baking soda, but an explosion, spewing fire and wrath. Our teacher was standing at the blackboard—chalk in one hand, eraser in the other, writing rows of arithmetic problems when the volcano erupted. She spun, faced the class, looked at me and exploded. Hot angry lava flowed from her mouth, onto the linoleum floor, onto my desk, onto me. I like to think I was only burned and not scarred.

I knew about volcanoes because during the summer my family had taken a day trip to the ancient volcanic field, west of Albuquerque. Volcanic forces over a million years ago had spewed hot molten lava, leaving their indelible imprint on the land forever. What was once lush desert is now known as the *malpais,* "bad lands." The terrain is stark, barren, and at times even eerie. It is important to stay on the narrow gravel path built by park rangers because on each side of the path are jagged black lava rocks, ready to trip and cut. Straying from the narrow path is dangerous.

My third grade class was a microcosm of the *malpais.* If I could have understood that concept, maybe the volcano would not erupted, maybe I would not have spent the year tripping and cutting myself on jagged rocks. But I was an eight-year-old child and headstrong. I did not know the cost of straying from the teacher's narrow path.

It began with my asking a simple arithmetic question. I was sitting at my desk. My mother had dressed me properly for school during those times. I wore a heavily starched dress with a sash that tied in the back. The dress was clean white, patterned with pink rose buds. I asked the teacher, "Why do we always add and subtract from right to left." The teacher said, "Because that is the way it is done." A child with any sense would have stopped there. I should have sat still in my desk and zipped my mouth shut. I was not that child. The pink rose buds on my desk burst to full bloom. I said, "But I want to do my arithmetic from left to right, like the way we read." The teacher ordered me to stand in the corner. The full-blown pink roses on my dress turned red with anger. I persisted, "But what is the answer to my question?"

The teacher erupted into a spewing volcano, dragging me to the principal's office to be hit with a paddle.

However, she was not satisfied with a beating. Every day she threw sharp ragged stones at me. I was sent to the corner so much I finally just put myself there at the beginning of school each day.

My legs hurt from standing all day, but other than that, the corner was actually not a bad place to spend third grade.

From the corner I could see the cloakroom where we hung our coats and scarves. The cloakroom was also the room where the three Native American children in our class had their desks. I do not know whether the teacher made them stay in the cloakroom; it could have been their choice. Maybe they had an understanding of volcanoes and knew to stay out of her way.

The children's names were Albert, Ethel, and James. We developed a unique relationship. We would whisper to each other and make hand signs when the teacher was not looking. After school they would play on the empty desert mesa across from the school. Sometimes I would join them. They taught me how to catch lizards. Ethel one day even showed me how to gently move a snake with a stick. She warned me, in a maternal voice, to never try it without her. She told me I was not an Indian and might not be able to recognize a dangerous snake that should be left alone.

One day I saw Albert sneak a small paper bag into the cloakroom with him. I thought it might be an apple or a candy bar, which of course was forbidden. It turned out to be a lizard. The lizard seemed content for a time to run across Albert's desk. Then the lizard suddenly darted from the cloakroom, slithered between the classroom desks and then with a bold leap landed on the teacher's shoe. She screamed and raised her hands. This movement lifted her skirt and revealed her slip underneath. I then understood everything. The slip should have been white but it was dingy.

My mother had taught me the meaning of dingy and what type of person wears dingy clothes. Laundry must be carefully sorted, bleached in Clorox, then hung on the clothes line in bright sunlight. It was crucial if a person were in an accident not to have dingy undergarments. If the ambulance drivers saw you had dingy underwear, they would know what type of person you were.

I never understood what "that type of person" was, but finally I was able to understand our teacher. She was a person with problems. A person with problems much greater than the microcosm of our classroom.

It saddens me, even now, that understanding does not always lead to forgiveness.

ANNIE OAKLEY TO THE RESCUE

It was fourth grade when the moon and stars aligned and a miracle happened. Annie Oakley came to Emerson Elementary School to teach. She was not the famous "sharpshooter" Annie Oakley, but a teacher. A good teacher. Everyone in our class felt like Cinderella on the day her Fairy Godmother arrived.

Mrs. Oakley saw each one of us as individuals with value. The Native American children left the cloakroom and joined the class. You could speak whatever language you wanted. She apologized for the fact that she spoke only English and sometimes mispronounced Spanish names.

She even allowed me to do my arithmetic from left to right. I soon learned that my method did not work when it came to carrying, that arithmetic is best done right to left. Mrs. Oakley understood children like me. She gave me an opportunity to try things my way. I figured out that many of my ideas didn't work and that Mrs. Oakley was teaching the class and me things for our benefit.

I only wish I had been old enough to fully realize and thank her for the gifts she gave me. I am hoping as I write this— that someone who is reading this knows Mrs. Oakley and tells her what a tremendous job she did as our teacher. She made a difference in my life and I am sure in every life she touched.

POLIO PIONEER

In 1954, third graders at Emerson Elementary School in Albuquerque stood in a line, rolled up our sleeves and saved thousands of children in our country from death and paralysis.

Albuquerque was one of only 215 test sites selected to determine the effectiveness of the Salk Vaccine against polio. In 1952, before the vaccine, there were 57,879 cases of paralytic polio resulting in 3,145 deaths. In 1960 after the introduction of the vaccine, there were only 3,140 cases and 230 deaths.

Polio was far more than a statistic to the children of our generation. One of my saddest memories as a child is of the five-year-old boy who lived across the street who contracted polio. He had to be moved from his bedroom, his toys, and his life into the family dining room. This was because it was the only room in his family's home that could accommodate his iron long. It was there he spent the last days of his short life, a little boy lying on his back, encased in a breathing machine.

Before the vaccine there was no effective way to prevent polio and little understanding of its epidemiology. Parents hoped that if their child contracted the disease that the devastation would be limited to leg braces and crutches. Mothers and fathers, not understanding the disease, did everything they could within their limited knowledge to protect their children from becoming a victim of polio. The disease was more prevalent during the summer, so many public swimming pools and Tingley Beach were closed. My mother thought perhaps it was the shock from going from the summer heat to the cold swimming pool water that brought on the disease. She filled my little back yard wading pool not with water from the hose, but with bucket after bucket of heated water from inside the house. My mother also thought, for some reason, that polio could be contracted from eating the portion of lettuce leaf that had turned brown. Her ideas may have been silly—but even today at age sixty-eight I cannot bring myself to swim in cold water or eat the brown part of a lettuce leaf. I understand the epidemiology of the disease, have been fully vaccinated, but I cannot erase from my mind a dining room with an iron lung and a little boy.

The work of developing the vaccine was the result of Jonas Salk's research, but it was made possible by the efforts of the people of our country as a whole. The March of Dimes headed up the funds for the fight against polio, raising research funds, literally one dime at a time. Once the vaccine was available, and Albuquerque was a selected site, mothers such as mine volunteered limitless hours putting everything in motion. I think my mother wore out two pairs of shoes going door to door to families of students explaining the test and collecting permission slips. Mom was there on shot day, with cotton balls and rubbing alcohol cleaning our arms, getting us ready for the shot that changed history.

Bataan Death March at the Kitchen Table

Flowered tablecloth

Company come to supper dishes

Lemonade and apple pie

I sit in my chair

age 8, patent leather shoes not touching floor

Hair braids, ribbon tied, ruffled yellow dress

small fingers clench as church looking for steeple

Edward has been invited to dinner

Edward is alive, but his body has been stolen

The Bataan Death March took it, leaving

his skin, thin translucent tissue paper

covering brittle battered bones

He trembles and stutters

His breath fast with shallow gasps

like a man near death

I plead with kitchen clock for dinner to end

It refuses, then whirls time backward

Japan imprisoning us in 1942

I do not want to look into Edward's eyes

fearing the deaths, the beatings, the starvation

I do not want to see Death March terror

the transitional phrase to our bombing Hiroshima

Japanese women screaming as flesh of babies burned

I make my eyes look into Edward's

His eyes do not hold the Death March

He is crying

for the babies

The March having only stolen his body

Lisa Myers

NIGHT IN THE DRUG STORE

Then there was the night my mother left me at Campbell Drug Store. She went to buy herself a carton of L&Ms, and I went along hoping she would buy me candy. When we got to the store, Mama remembered we were at the very end of the toothpaste tube, so she took a box of Pepsodent off the shelf. Together we walked up to the front counter so she could get her cigarettes and pay.

"How are you, Betty?" asked Mrs. Campbell.

I stood there gazing at all the candy laid out in neat rows. Did I want a candy bar...a Butterfinger or a Three Musketeers? Was I more in the mood for a Chick-O-Stick? A candy necklace was always a good choice.

"Oh, I'm okay," said Mama. "It's very busy now that school has started again. The first day I had 26 students and only 22 desks."

Maybe I should get a package of Necco Wafers. I picked up different items and put them back down. I finally decided on a package of SweeTarts. I handed them to Mama and asked, "Can I go look at the toys?"

"I'm not buying you a thing," she said, but she nodded

her head. The two of them were still chatting as I walked away. I looked at the toys for a long time. So long I began wondering what they could possibly be talking about. I went back up to the front of the store. Mrs. Campbell wasn't there. Behind the counter, Mr. Campbell was ringing up a customer. My mother wasn't there.

I knew then she left without me, but I refused to believe it. First, I went straight back to the toys thinking she came to get me and we missed one another as I went back to her. When she wasn't there, I thought maybe she went to the bathroom. I hurried to the back of the store. The door to the bathroom was wide open. She wasn't getting a drink at the water fountain either. I went back up to the front counter. No, she was not still visiting with Mrs. Campbell. I felt the fear rise in me.

What should I do? My mother went off and left me. Then it occurred to me she might be waiting for me in the car. I went outside, and the spot where we parked was empty. When we came, it wasn't dark, but now the HOFFMANTOWN SHOPPING CENTER sign was lit up. The fear inside me became panic. My heart flew up. My stomach churned. I was close to tears. I went back inside. There was nothing I hated more than having to ask for help. Even though I was only 5 years old, I was determined to figure out how to get home without having to admit I needed help. I considered walking, but I wasn't allowed to cross Menaul alone—it was a busy street with two lanes on each side of the divider. And it was too far to walk all the way home in the dark without one of my sisters anyway. I didn't have a dime to use the pay phone. I went one more time to the toy aisle just in case.

I found Mrs. Campbell behind the cosmetics counter, and I stood there, silent. The smell of perfume was heavy in the air. I thought I might vomit. "Oh, dear," Mrs. Campbell said. She came out from behind the counter and put her hand on my shoulder. And then she called my mother.

I chewed the inside of my mouth as I listened to Mrs. Campbell's side of the phone conversation.

"May I speak with your mother?"

"Betty, Lisa is here."

"Okay, that's good."

After she hung up, Mrs. Campbell took me by the hand and said, "She's on her way." She walked me back to the red vinyl sofa near the prescription counter where I sat down and waited. Mr. Campbell came over and gave me a lime Dum Dum. He smiled at me but did not say a word. I traced the cracks in the vinyl. I ate the sucker even though I didn't like anything lime flavored. I even ate the paper stick. The wire spinner rack with comics was near, but I didn't dare move to go look at them. It was an eternity before I saw my sister, Beth.

My mother didn't come inside and get me herself. She

sent Beth in. "Thank you, "Beth said to Mr. Campbell. We walked through the store and out to the car. The tears came when I saw both Karen and Lynn waiting in the car. Mother had her window rolled down, and she was smoking one of her newly purchased cigarettes. Karen was already laughing when I crawled into the middle of the back seat. She turned around, leaned way over the seat, waggled her finger at me and said, "I tried to tell Mother she should just leave you here."

"Yeah," Lynn said, "the Campbells don't have any kids of their own, but they definitely wouldn't want you!" Mother said nothing. She took us all to Peter Pan's Drive-In for cherry limeades and tater tots.

Maria Leyba

Al-Lah and 1,000 Signs of the Cross

Finally, after four years away from *mi querido barrio,* we were coming home. Released from the claustrophobic desert and life behind barbed wires with guards watching our every move, I was ecstatic! I would never again have to ride the school bus to Santa Fe and be known as the "Penitentiary Kid."

Barelas seemed like heaven to me! I made a list of all the things I would be doing, like walking to school, playing outside without guards watching; but most of all I would have real friends.

My barrio was full of little girls my age and I could hardly wait to explore this new chapter in my young life. Mama took us to register at Coronado Elementary School; my brothers and I were excited to be taken to our new classrooms. I couldn't believe it— my classroom was on the second floor facing 4th Street! I had never been in a room with such beautiful wood floors, and instead of our own desks we sat at tables. After testing me my new teacher, Ms. Hudson, proclaimed I would be sitting at the smart table in front of the class.

The four boys already sitting there just glared at me. I wondered why no girls were sitting at the smart table. I attributed it to finally having a good command of the English language.

I soon learned that my brothers and I were the only children in school with Spanish names that had not been changed into English. My oldest brother strongly objected to having our names changed and so we clung to our Spanish names like our life depended on it.

During recess I realized that not too many kids were talking to me. Some of the boys called me "Four eyes," "Daddy long legs" or "Bookworm." When I responded in Spanish the children's eyes grew wide, shocked that I was fluent in Spanish. Some of the boys even said, " *Hijola la* bookworm can speak Spanish!"

At this school no one got mad if we spoke Spanish during recess and just hearing other children speaking my language was so heartwarming. I had never been so happy in my life!

This barrio was bursting with colors, life and sounds like none I had ever heard. I was madly in love with my new world and counted my blessings every day. No one had to tell me to wake up in the morning, just hearing the birds singing and children's voices outside sent me spinning, dying to discover another day.

The first time when I was in my classroom and a fire truck drove by with the siren blaring, most of the class started making signs of the cross; it seemed like 1,000. I had never witnessed anything like that and soon came to realize that they made signs of the cross when policemen or ambulances roared by on 4th Street. When they walked in front of Sacred Heart Church they did the same thing. Some kids accused me of not being Catholic but a Russian Communist. They said my mama was an ex-Hungarian actress; in their minds that was close to Russia. I soon joined the "1,000 cross" children every Monday after school for catechism class at Sacred Heart School right across from Coronado School. I thought the nuns were so strict and the nuns thought I was an inferior heathen.

My heart sank when I realized that Ms. Hudson never picked on the smart table to harass or mistreat. That was reserved for the children who sat at the dumb table. She made sure that those unfortunate children sat in the back, so when she called on them we could all turn around to stare at their disgrace.

Ms. Hudson was a very old teacher who lived alone and looked like a witch. She loved to pick on Joe, a 12-year-old still in fourth grade. She became rabidly insane because when she picked on Joe, he never said a word. He just stood there stoically while she beat him, demanding that he cry. But he never did! The rest of class was instructed to lay our heads on the table and not look, as if that made it okay. The first time I witnessed the abuse I wanted to cry but instead made 1,000 signs of the cross like the rest of the children.

Rita, my best friend, soon became Ms. Hudson's next target. Rita was terrified of public speaking and Ms. Hudson was forcing her to stand up in front of the class and give a short report. Calling her all sorts of very demeaning words when Rita stood silently. My heart broke just watching Rita trying so hard to open her mouth. I kept wishing something would come out—anything! But she just couldn't do it. Ms. Hudson was furious and just kept saying, "Why are you Mexican kids so stubborn!" When the school bell rang she made Rita stay inside while the rest of us where ordered to leave. I waited outside for Rita by the school gate; after a short while she came out running and crying. She couldn't say anything just lifted her skirt to show me the black and blue bruises on her thighs. Our eyes locked and we both knew what had happened. All I could say was, Al - lah!

Lola's Garden

My parched throat became unbearable the summer of my tenth year. A mysterious dark cloud pursued me at every corner and at night I could not chase the nightmares away. Ms. Hudson was now well behind me, and in the fall I would have a new teacher. How I prayed for a teacher that would be nice to all the children! Still I couldn't understand why melancholy thick as dust draped my dejected shoulders.

In the middle of summer I was walking to the Barelas Community Center thinking of the little birds singing up in the trees overhead. When I heard a delicate yet familiar voice, I followed that sound past the morning glories and roses. The woman with the delightful voice was firmly planted in the middle of her garden smiling from ear to ear while watering. Then unexpectedly she sprayed me with the water hose and said, "You looked like you needed to be refreshed." We both just looked at each other and started laughing in a way I hadn't done in a long time.

I was transfixed, swallowed whole into Lola's luminous black eyes and absorbed into her velvet mahogany skin that lay taut against her high cheekbones. I envied her glorious black hair coiled loosely into a bun. I felt too pale and plain next to this marvelous Aztec Goddess. But it was her laughter that exploded and rippled from deep inside her that told me she would be the medium to fuse my past and future. Her garden would become my refuge when I needed to hear ancient chants to calm my jitterish nerves to soothe my wounded young heart.

Sometimes Lola nudged me into her warm womb nestled between her table and stove. She would serve me *atole* from the simmering pot she kept on the back burner of her white stove; the same one she used to feed her own children. Other times she would open the trapdoor in the kitchen and I would follow her childish enthusiasm down the creaky dusty stairs in search of treasures hidden in adobe walls.

Her *casita* was my perfect sanctuary where she gradually transformed me and became the best teacher I would ever have. Some days I just wanted to stare at the art her son Juan had created. Lola hung his canvases on her white blank walls. They were beautiful, brilliant colorful modern art that just fascinated me. Juan's fertile imagination stirred something in me that I had no name for. Her oldest daughter, Eleanor, was an excellent seamstress and loved to take us for rides in her Volvo. One Monday morning she took her little sister Rosie and me to the public library on Edith. I had never been to a library; not even the school I attended had a library. I was ecstatic and couldn't believe my good luck at being able to take all those books home to read!

Throughout my childhood and teens I would go

knocking on Lola's wooden door with a glass section at the top. I would wait patiently for her shadow to scurry across the wooden floor and watch her slender fingers pull back the lace white curtain to see who was knocking. I was always welcomed with so much warmth and love. Eagerly I sat on her floral chair across from her, waiting for this enchanting storyteller to take me to magical places.

I still take my daily morning walks and purposely pass by Lola's old garden. It's all gone now, all the houses on her block were demolished by the city in the late seventies. They called it progress and wanted to make space for ugly senior housing with teeny tiny yards.

If I close my eyes I can see Lola's garden and *casita* humming alongside the unending city noises. I can almost hear her musical laughter and feel her enthusiasm. This beautiful brown woman who rescued me from my childish despair and taught me to grow and heal in Lola's Garden.

JUNE 1958

Lynn Ewing

LOUIS THE BREAD MAN

My mother didn't drive. She had things delivered to the house. On summer days when we were home, my brothers and I were accustomed to answering the door to accept her prescriptions from the pharmacy, gin and wine from the liquor store, dry cleaning and staples packaged in the distinctive gold and brown packaging from the Jewel T man. Like everyone else, we had the milkman deliver milk, cream, cottage cheese and other dairy products early in the morning twice a week. So it was no surprise when one summer afternoon, there was a knock at the door and I answered it to find a man who immediately called out in honeyed southern drawl, "Yoohoo, bread man." He was a large, open-faced man with golden hair and friendly blue eyes.

I called down the hall to Mom, who was in bed reading, and invited Louis in. As my brothers, mother and I gathered around him in the living room, Louis told us he and his wife had just moved to Albuquerque from New Orleans for his wife's health. He was familiar with Albuquerque, having been stationed at Sandia Base briefly during the war. Louis had just opened a bakery and was offering home delivery. He handed out samples of cookies and breads to my brothers and me and we were hooked. After telling us about himself, Louis took an order from Mom and promised to deliver the order two days later. He finished his glass of mint iced tea, a staple in our house, and asked us about ourselves, then left with a smiling, drawled, "Your bread man will see y'all soon," and left.

When Louis returned two days later, he had everything Mom had ordered, plus a loaf of bread shaped like a turtle for me. He had remembered me telling him that I loved turtles and made it specially for "turtle girl," as he insisted on calling me forever after. Each week, Louis arrived at the front door, called out "Yoohoo, bread man," and carried in a basket overflowing with baked goods Mom had ordered and special treats for us kids. Mine was always a turtle loaf of bread, but each week, Louis varied the expression on the turtle's face. One week there would be a grin, the next week a frown and the next week, one eyebrow raised suspiciously. My brothers and I loved Louis. What energy and love he had left after baking he poured into us when he visited. We looked forward to delivery days and made sure we were home to greet him and hear his stories. Louis described the streets of New Orleans, filled with flowers of every possible color, people heading from one party to another walking in time to the jazz wafting out the doors of bars and clubs. He'd finish a story and say, "Y'all would love it, especially you, turtle girl."

Louis baked Christmas tree coffee cakes at Christmas and introduced us to King Cake during Mardi Gras. At Easter, we had bunny bread and tulip cookies, and the tales of life in the South continued to hypnotize us.

One day, Louis didn't arrive in the afternoon. Mom told us he had probably gotten too busy and not to worry about it. Dad got home from work, tense and snappish, and we sat down to dinner with the TV flashing black and white pictures of the Vietnam War and protests. As my brothers and I sat eating quietly, rushing to get the meal done so we could run outside to play, we heard a knock at the front door, then heard the door open a bit followed by, "Yoohoo, bread man." Dad glared at us kids and yelled, "You kids knock off the g-d noise right now." We just stared at him. We had been sitting right there quietly where he could see us. Our lips had not moved. Did he think while he was at work we had practiced for hours and become talented ventriloquists like Shari Lewis? Mom left the table and brought Louis back for Dad to meet. He joined us at the table and he and Dad got to know each other over martinis. My brothers and I gladly left the table and headed outside while Louis charmed Dad and left our treats.

Louis became a fixture at our house for the next two and half years. On Saturdays Dad would frequently take us to Louis' bakery where we could watch him work his magic in flour, sugar and butter. Mom and Dad had Louis and his wife to dinner and went to dinner at their house. My brothers and I knew that on delivery days, we would each receive some special little gift from Louis and we'd race home from school to see what he had left for us.

One Tuesday in late February, my brothers and I shoved our way through the door to see what Louis had left for us. Nothing was there. Mom was sitting at the kitchen counter crying. She had just heard Louis had an inoperable brain tumor.

We never saw Louis again, never got to say goodbye or thank you. We missed his thoughtful treats, the crusty bread for our sandwiches, my turtle bread and the pastries. But what we missed most was the man whose honeyed drawl and big personality burst into our lives one summer afternoon with the greeting, "Yoohoo, bread man."

The Day After Thanksgiving

Thanksgiving might have been one of my parents' favorite holidays when my brothers and I were young children. When the day arrived, we three rushed to do anything asked of us with big smiles and cheerful attitudes. Beds were made without reminders. The table was set, potatoes were peeled. The front walk was swept, all without a single complaint.

Added to that was the fact that we managed not to bicker or fight for an entire day. I even ate pumpkin pie without complaining. I mean, we worked hard to be the best kids in the world on Thanksgiving Day. My parents may have thought it was because our aunt, uncle, grandmother and grandfather as well as family friends were there and we were trying to show off for them. They may have congratulated themselves that their impeccable parenting style was at long last paying off. They would have been wrong. We were good because we knew that the next day, after the big Christmas Parade in downtown Albuquerque, we would be going into Fedway to stand in line behind hundreds of other children to tell Santa Claus what we wanted for Christmas.

Fedway was one of the major department stores downtown. It was made exotic by virtue of the fact that the parking lot was on the roof. My brothers and I were well acquainted with Fedway because our aunt took us on frequent shopping expeditions with her. We loved driving up the steep ramp to the roof of the building where Jeany would park her car and head to the door. Inside the door from the parking lot was the candy counter. It was the only thing in the entry area from the parking lot and beckoned to my brothers and me with alluring smells of chocolate and seductive hard candies spinning on a crystal plate behind the glass counter.

After passing the candy counter wistfully, longingly, we would turn right and go down the escalator into the main part of the store. We would follow Jeany around as she tried on shoes and dresses or picked out gifts for friends' birthdays and anniversaries. Jeany was a master shopper if ever there was one and we loved being with her as she pursued the perfect purchase.

On the day after Thanksgiving, the entire family would dress in layers, pile into the car and head downtown. We tried to get there early enough to get good seats to watch the parade. Mom would pass around cups of hot chocolate from a thermos and we'd drink hot chocolate, eat donuts and ask every two seconds, "When is it going to start?"

Finally, the parade would begin. We would be dazzled by baton twirling teenage girls from Albuquerque High School leading the school band down the street. Following them came the trained poodles, all dressed up in tutus or fiesta skirts and prancing on their hind legs in time to the music. Wave after wave of high school bands entertained us, along with tiny cars overflowing with clowns who would jump out and throw candy at us. The big attraction, at least for most children at the parade, was at the end. Santa Claus in his sleigh would glide by, smiling and waving at all the spectators.

For me, the main attraction was our friend Perry, who rode a tall unicycle just in front of Santa's sleigh. My memory of the unicycle is that it was taller than the buildings. No doubt that is a trick of memory, but it truly was a very tall unicycle. What made this thrilling to me was that Perry always kept an eye out for my brothers and me and made a point of riding over to us and calling our names. It was our yearly 15 seconds of fame and I basked in it. Once Perry had passed by, I tried to urge my brothers and parents to start heading to Fedway so we could catch Santa Claus before all the other kids wore him out with their demands. No matter how hard I tried to get us there quickly, there was always a long line to wait in. We used the wait to go over our greedy little lists of things we planned to ask for in spite of the fact that we knew Santa only gave us one gift each year.

One year, after the parade, we were invited to visit some friends of my aunt and uncle. They were an older couple who lived in the country club area. He was a retired General. They had met when he was in the hospital with a terrible injury during WWII. She was a nun who was his nurse in that hospital. He fell in love with her and convinced her to leave the order and marry him.

My brothers were very excited about this invitation. I didn't understand why they were so excited. These people didn't have children for us to play with and I liked the ex-nun, but wasn't all that impressed with the General, who made a big deal out of being a retired General. After the usual greetings took place, the General took my brothers out to his garage to show them something. I stayed inside with the tea and cookies. I couldn't imagine what could be that exciting in a garage. After about ten minutes, my brothers came in and grabbed me and said, "The General is going to take us for a ride. Come on." I wanted to refuse, but my parents sent me out. I got in the car grudgingly and the General drove us around town for about an hour. My brothers were touching the seats and looking at the dashboard and making all kinds of comments that were of no interest to me. After an hour, the General turned into his driveway and let us out where our parents were waiting for us. We thanked him for the ride and thanked his wife for her hospitality and headed home. All the way home, my brothers talked non-stop about the wonderful General and his wonderful car. They said, "And did you know he has two of them? One for his wife and one for himself." I just let them ramble on and wondered to myself what the big deal was. Okay, so he had two cars and we had ridden in one of them. So what?

When I couldn't take it anymore, I asked why they were so excited about riding around in a car. It wasn't exactly the first time the three of us had been in a car. The entire family stared at me in amazement. "You just rode around town in a Rolls Royce!" my mother exclaimed. "How many people ever get to do that?" I still didn't see what the big deal was. After all, it was a car. It had four wheels and went forward and backward. Who cares? My brothers just shook their heads in disgust and went back to their rhapsodies about the General and his car. They said it was one of the best days of their lives.

I hated to tell them, but the thing that made it the best day of our lives was not the car, it was Perry riding his unicycle up to us and calling our names. Now *that* was worth something!

THE FIRES OF JULY

"Oh, crap! Get the hose! Don't let Dad know!" My older brother has put us on high alert as the aromas of sulfur and burning weeds fill the air. Once again, it's the Fourth of July and we have set the mesa next to our parent's house on fire. It's tradition. What else would healthy teenagers do on the Fourth of July but play with fire and cause fires?

My older brother loved pyrotechnics like nobody's business. From the time he was ten, Brian had sources for illegal fireworks. We always had bottle rockets, firecrackers and roman candles. Of course, they were illegal. Of course, they were dangerous. That's why he loved them and shared that love with our younger brother and me.

Each year Brian would save money, charm/coerce money from us and go get the fireworks. When the Fourth arrived, he had a stash worthy of a professional show. The day would start with us helping get the house ready for the annual July Fourth party. We'd dust, vacuum, clean the patio, hang lanterns across the patio, set up tables and chairs and help our mother with the cooking. By 3:00 p.m. our parents were usually showered, changed and sipping martinis in preparation for their guests.

My brothers and I would head outside. We'd start with a

bottle rocket. At first, that was fun. Soon, however, we'd decide to wire 10 bottle rockets together and set them off. That would become old hat and we'd see if we could wire more together and launch them from our hands without getting hurt.

It usually happened about 5:00 p.m. Friends and neighbors would be arriving and Mom and Dad would be busy handing out cocktails and hors d'oeuvres to the neurosurgeon from Guatemala, the TV station manager, the artist, while any children were sent to find us where we'd still be outside setting off bottle rockets. It never failed that one of us would notice dry grass and tumble weeds ablaze and start shouting, "Oh crap! Get the hose! Don't let Dad know!" And there we'd go, the three stooges of Sunningdale Drive grabbing the hose, buckets, and shovels, and running in all directions until the fire was out and disaster was diverted.

Our love of the Fourth of July spectacle was engrained early in our lives. From the time we were toddlers until we were in grade school, our celebrations started first thing in the morning and ended with a big fireworks show—a professional fireworks show, but with a fire truck at the ready and frequently used.

Back then, we'd wake up and get into our swimsuits right away. The entire family would pile in the car and we'd head to the Officer's Club at Sandia Base. Once there, our parents would get us situated at the children's activities and head off to find friends and start their party. We would spend the day in the swimming pool, diving for pennies, having races and diving contests, and running occasionally to the snack bar for French fries and Cokes to fuel our water play.

Around dinnertime, we were all herded to the locker rooms to shower and change into the nice clothes our parents had packed for us. We girls had sundresses and sandals. The boys wore short-sleeved shirts with ties and dress pants. We'd comb our hair, roll our soggy swimsuits in towels and head inside to join our parents in the cocktail lounge, adding the smell of chlorine to the aroma of cigarettes, perfume and whiskey already pervading the room. The adults would continue with their martinis and manhattans and we'd get Shirley Temples and beg the bartender for extra cherries or better yet, get the cherries out of someone's manhattan. Now *that* was a good cherry!

Eventually, the entire group, usually about twenty of us, would head to the buffet, my favorite place. We had a selection of cheeses, breads, olives, and pickles followed by salads of every kind imaginable. Next on the table were chilled poached salmon, fried chicken, rice, potatoes and a steamship round of beef sliced to order. Oh, I loved that buffet and always went back for seconds and even thirds. There was a separate table of desserts too. As we stuffed ourselves, a jazz quartet would begin to play and the adults would get up to dance. My brothers and I were expected to dance with each other and with any adults who offered to dance with us. I didn't mind this so much but my brothers hated it. They just wanted to get outside and wait for the big show.

Once it was dark, everyone in the club would head back out to the pool area and await the fireworks. The Officer's Club put on a spectacular show every year. Part of the fun for me was hearing everyone oooh and aaah simultaneously with each new explosion of color and sparks. Equally exciting were the times the area behind the wall caught fire and we got to see the firemen at work putting out the flames.

We'd finally head home about 11:00 o'clock. We kids would be exhausted, sunburned and well fed, ready to sleep. Our parents would be well lubricated and well fed and ready to sleep.

The first time our parents told us we were not going to the Club, but would be having a Fourth of July party at home, I'm pretty sure that we thought they were proposing something not only illegal but un-American. How could we have the Fourth of July without the fireworks show, the buffet, the swimming pool?

Ever the problem solver, Brian soon learned where and how to obtain fireworks and we were off and running. Our parents and many of their guests purchased legal fireworks at the grocery store and we had those, but they just didn't pack the wallop of the illegal ones. I enjoyed setting the snakes on fire on the sidewalk during the day and inhaling the sulfurous fumes, but that didn't come close to what a bottle rocket could do. I enjoyed the fountains that were legal, but they just weren't roman candles. And so our careers as pyromaniacs began.

When I remember those celebrations and the annual fires, I wonder why we were surprised by the fires each year. We must have secretly enjoyed the adrenaline rush of racing to put out the flames without being caught. Anyway, we always enjoyed our Fires of July.

THE MAN IN THE LEATHER GLOVES

When I was eight, my mother started singing in the choir at Immanuel Presbyterian Church in Nob Hill. As a result, I started attending church with her. I had no interest in attending Sunday School. Not for me, coloring pictures and drinking watered-down Kool-Aid. I wanted to be where the action was, in the sanctuary with the grown-ups.

Lest you arrive at the conclusion that I was a highly spiritual child, let me correct that notion. I did like the music and the candles, but my favorite thing about going to church was getting all dressed up and being the only kid in church, thus garnering lots of approving glances and smiles. I loved showing up in my hats made by my mother to match my dresses, my white gloves and patent leather Mary Janes. I enjoyed "looking" like a good girl without having to go to the trouble of actually being one.

I soon discovered that the best place to be in church was in the balcony. When I sat up there I was usually alone, free to command the entire area. I could see my mother up in the choir loft at the opposite end of the church as well as watch the other members of the congregation during the service. From the balcony, I was in the know about who failed to bow their head in prayer and which people didn't even bother to open their hymnals when it was time to sing. I felt like a queen surveying her subjects up there.

One Sunday, after leaving my mother in the choir rehearsal room in the basement of the church, I made my way to my usual spot in the balcony. Just before the service began, a man about my parents' age arrived in the balcony and sat a few pews behind me. What stood out about his appearance was that he wore black leather gloves and never took them off. As the service progressed, I occasionally heard the man talking softly behind me. He was alone and he certainly wasn't talking to me, so I thought he must be praying out loud. When the service ended I raced down to meet my mother in front of the church where my father would be parked to pick us up and take us home to a big Sunday dinner.

The following Sunday I followed the same routine, arriving in the balcony and carefully choosing my seat before the choir lined up to proceed down the center aisle. Once again, the man in the leather gloves took a seat a few pews behind me and talked softly throughout the service.

This had continued for several weeks when I mentioned it to my parents on the way home from church one Sunday. I just thought the man was a curiosity. I wasn't concerned, as he never seemed to notice I was in the balcony with him. My father thought maybe I should stop going to the balcony, but I assured him that there was no need for me to change my habit.

Then came the Sunday when the man sat right next to me and talked to himself throughout the service. What I had not known with him sitting behind me and speaking softly was that his talk was about, "them" and "getting away from them" and that the entire time he talked, he stroked his left hand with his right one. This made me a little uncomfortable, but I didn't want to move away from him on the pew and risk hurting his feelings. Besides, it wasn't as if his talking was preventing me from listening to the sermon. I always daydreamed during the sermon, anyway.

"Why didn't you move away from that man?" my mother questioned me as soon as we met in front of the church. "You've got to stop sitting the in balcony with him."

"Why? What could possibly happen in front of hundreds of people in church in broad daylight?" I asked her. Without responding, she got in the car and I followed. We said no more on the subject.

That week, I thought about the man in the leather gloves a lot. I wondered who "they" were and why he needed to get away from "them." When Sunday rolled around once again, I left Mom in the rehearsal hall as usual, but instead of heading straight to the balcony, I hunted for my piano teacher, who was a longtime member of the church. I found her having coffee and chatting with friends in the church parlor and asked her if she knew anything about my new church companion. She said she didn't know him, but would ask around and let me know what she found out. Then I headed to the balcony and the man with the leather gloves was sitting in MY pew. Rather than go to another seat, I decided I'd sit next to him. I smiled at him as I sat down and listened as he spoke softly again about "them" and stroked his left hand with his right one.

Two weeks later, my piano teacher kept me a few minutes after my lesson to explain what she had learned about the man in the leather gloves. He had been in the Bataan Death March during WWII and had lost a hand. He wore gloves on both hands to hide a prosthetic hand as well as scars on the other hand. She told me that I should read more about the Bataan Death March so that I could understand what he had been through and how it had affected his mind. I left her house with lofty ideas about how I was going to befriend the man and help him get better. Those ideas never panned out, as my piano teacher shared her information with my parents, who laid down the law and forbade me sitting in the balcony ever again. That was the end of my childhood church career. I decided to stay home and read on Sundays instead, leaving the balcony to the man in the leather gloves.

Cynthia Sylvester

Two Crows Laughing

Some families are like grand oaks that grow steadfast in the same place, generation after generation. Others are like weeds, tumbling and crashing into each other, disintegrating, to rise again the following summer without any nurturing and just a whisper of a prayer. Some families are like roses grown in the desert, requiring laughter to make them real.

When I was a kid my bedroom window faced east, the sun illuminating the small room I shared with my older sister. The drapes, special ordered from JC Penney, glowed like an orange soda, like contentment.

But contentment, akin to peace, is fragile, much like the desert floor that can become a torrent of water during monsoon season, lightning and ozone all that's left behind of what had been planted. When disaster strikes and wipes out your fields, your home, where do you find the strength to plant again? Who do you speak to, the sun or the moon?

I got the answer as I was sitting on the edge of the hot walkway in front of our house in my cheap drugstore sunglasses staring at the sun, daring her to blind me. A gust of wind blew sand in my face and then whispered in my ear, "Don't let it die."

I looked around. On the porch in black containers were

two rose bushes my mom had bought weeks, maybe months ago. Occasionally I would give them water and return to sitting on the edge of the walkway, my toes curled up in the dead grass. I thought of the old tiller my dad had left behind, then eyed the spot where we had thought of planting them beneath my bedroom window—now a patch of hardened soil since the rain gutters had fallen off the house.

I got up and dragged the tiller from the garage and down the cement walk. We sounded like a metal demon, a storm on the mesa. Mom came to the front door and asked what I was doing?

"It's time," I said. "We've got to plant those rose bushes, they're gonna die."

She studied the old Sears tiller. Rusted, naturally decayed, cocked to one side, it looked dangerous and harmless at the same time.

She came outside, taking hold of one handle and I the other, and we completed our procession to the small patch below the window. I checked the tiller for gas, then pulled the drawstring over and over. Sun watched us from a distance as we took turns trying to start it until our skinny arms burned and we gasped for air.

Wind came up, blew sand in our eyes, and yelled, "Open the choke."

Mom flipped the switch, I pulled the string and the old tiller sputtered to life.

We looked at each other. "Flaps up," I said, and pushed the throttle all the way down. The tiller lurched forward, dragging us behind it. It was like a wild mustang, glad to be out of the corral, knocking us off the handles, and jumping wildly from hard packed ground to house, kicking up dust and tearing the stucco off the wall.

Choking on exhaust, I got hold of the handles and yelled over the noise, "Disengage the engine!"

I looked at her, my co-pilot, doubled over with laughter. "Mom, flaps down!" She reached the lever. The tiller sputtered, shook one last time, coughed, and died. I pulled my sunglasses off. Rings of dirt surrounded my eyes, which only made Mom laugh harder. I stared at the holes in the side of the house, horrified at the damage we had caused. If Dad were here, he'd kill us.

But he wasn't here.

Then slowly, something akin to sadness rose up in me and erupted painfully into laughter.

Finally, she looked at me and without a word went back to the garage, got the shovel and began digging. Sun pulled a cloud over her face as we dug two holes, wide enough and deep enough for our rose bushes. We poured water in the holes and watched it seep slowly into the soil. It was a grand burial, the smell of moist soil rising like smoke, as we patted the ground. For years we had so many roses, at times the branches sagged with the weight of their grace.

And still on some hot summer days when the wind begins to blow, I wonder what it's saying? Maybe nothing, maybe it's just blowing a memory back to me, of us standing in the desert, laughing like two black crows. Laughing just to laugh, again.

LEGEND OF THE HIGH NOON MOON

Every summer our tribe held a race to see which clan could fly the fastest and farthest. Under section C, article twelve, of the Fourth Sacred Law, it clearly stated that: The People can fly, but only on shields and *only* when the moon is full. The exception was the Sparrow Clan, who were to be the referees of the race.

The Bat Clan had won the race for the past 300 years. This made the Antelope Clan very angry, for they were known for quick action and athletic ability. They couldn't see how the Bats—comprised primarily of old women who sat around in the dark telling stories and smoking pipes—could beat them year after year. The more they thought about it, the more it became clear that the Bats were cheating. So they would too. The Antelopes got together with Coyote and made a plan.

It was high noon in the middle of the hottest day of the year. The Sparrows sat in a piñon tree at the base of the Fourth Sacred Mountain eating nuts. The Antelopes came out of their hogan with their flying shields. They sat down on the dirt road and waited for the moon to come up. The Bats were in their hogan, sipping coffee, smoking pipes and talking about all the races they'd won over the years. The Bats weren't worried because they were good friends with Sister Moon. They'd give her some tobacco and she'd tell them just exactly when she'd be arriving.

So when the moon came up and sat on top of the mountain in the middle of the day, it was a big surprise. The chief of the Sparrow Clan spit out a nut and yelled, "Let the race begin."

The Antelopes took off on their shields, rising swiftly until they were only specks in the blue summer sky. The Sparrows flew into the Bats' hogan. It was so filled with smoke and so dark they could barely see. They told the Bats, "The moon is out. The Antelopes are winning the race."

The Bats, not expecting to fly for another four nights, readied themselves by making another pot of coffee.

Meanwhile the rest of the tribe, comprised of the Spider Clan and the Lizard Clan, who had forgotten how to fly a long time ago, gathered around to look up into the sky. They marveled at how quickly the young Antelopes were traveling. They began to gossip about the Bats, saying that they were too old and had begun to make mistakes.

The sun was setting when the Bats finally came out. They looked to the top of Sacred Mountain Number Four and said, "If that's the moon, why is the sun setting right next to it?"

The People went silent. The Bats were right. That wasn't

the moon. The Antelopes and Coyote had tricked them. They'd stolen the sacred shield from Grandfather's hogan. Crafty Coyote used a piece of mica to reflect the sun so that the old, nearly transparent hide of the shield looked like a summer moon atop the mountain. They thought they were pretty clever until the sacred shield and Coyote's tail caught fire. Coyote howled and howled.

In fact, he's still howling at the Antelopes about his burnt tail.

The young Antelopes never made it any farther. They were frozen into stars in the northern sky—frozen in the shape of a bat. A reminder of what can happen if the sacred laws are broken. A reminder to always, always listen like an old Bat.

Georgia Santa Maria

LITERACY STORY

When I was two years old, I started college. I went to the University of New Mexico's Childcare Center that was down the street from my grandparents' house, where my mother and I lived. I will never forget my first day at school. I came down the slide and skinned my knee, bled all over and wrecked my new dress. I cried buckets. There was snot and tears and blood everywhere, and I decided right then that school was not going to be for me. I hated it. When I couldn't stop crying and pleading to go home, the teacher got mad at me and shouted at me, saying I was being "bad." Then we drank orange juice, which she seemed to think was a real treat, but I hiccoughed and it came up the back of my throat into my nose and really hurt, so I cried even harder, which made her even madder.

One of the auspices of the Childcare Center in those days was experimental psychology. They were frequently "observing our behavior" and giving us newly devised IQ tests, etc. I regarded this as both amusing and insulting: nobody asked me if I wanted to be somebody's guinea pig! At age four or so, I enjoyed as much as possible the prospect of messing up their data by being outrageous and unpredictable. I took on the role of McMurphy in *One Flew Over The Cuckoo's Nest*. I was seditious. I told the other kids to be uncooperative and say surprising things to their stupid questions. I was labeled "A Behavior Problem." I was officially no longer a person. I was a problem to be solved. The teachers shook their heads and said to my mother, "We just don't know what we're going to do with Georgia!" My mother concurred and spanked me good and hard. But honestly, by then, the only fun I was having in school was confounding the "experts."

At home I had a wonderful imagination. I played fantastic roles. My favorite was wild Apache, hair flying, my bow and arrows at the ready, I wanted to be Geronimo. Kill the psychologists and burn their clinic. Raze the school and scalp my teachers.

When I started first grade at Emerson Elementary we had just moved. My mother had just married my new stepfather, who seemed like a nice enough bloke, but didn't really have much of a feel for fatherhood yet. I think he was a little afraid of me. I remember he wanted to teach me to fish. I fell into a wasp's nest and got stung all over, and he put mud on the stings so they would stop hurting. That made me feel a little better about him—the cool mud was great, and he didn't let it bother him that it was messy or stinky—he just wanted to stop the hurting.

Emerson seemed to be governed by a lot of rules and punishments for breaking them. I got spanked with a ping-pong paddle for going to the bathroom during recess, which wasn't allowed. A friend had let me into the building. Mrs. Jones paddled me publicly and encouraged the other children to enjoy the spectacle. When I cried she ridiculed me, calling me "cry baby," and getting the other children to chime in.

Mrs. Jones was a bit of a Nazi. She had her favorites, usually boys, and she thought little girls should be "nice," which meant invisible. Tommy was her favorite, a little blonde boy who was the best reader in the class. She graded reading by behavioral standards. If you misbehaved, she put you back into a lower reading group in order to humiliate you and let the other kids know you were bad and stupid. I was in the lowest reading group—so low that there wasn't anybody else in it with me. Tommy was one of a kind at the top and I was at the bottom. I was bad and stupid. I figured why try? The books were full of good little children who always did what they were told. Reading about them seemed boring and dumb. "See Spot run." Who cares? I'd rather be bad. My first report card had all F's on it. I got spanked again. School was Hell.

I hung out with Richard Gonzales, who was labeled a *Pachuco* because he wore his older brother's baggy pants and spoke Spanish and ate tortillas and jam for lunch. Richard was bad too. He wasn't even in any reading group. Everybody knew Richard was going to grow up to be a criminal. I thought he was super cool! Even Mrs. Jones didn't have it over Richard. Nobody could make him cry. He would just give them one of his murderous dark looks, and they'd leave him alone. I practiced murderous dark looks of my own, but I was never as good at it as Richard.

I spent my life in the Principal's office. Mrs. Martin said, "In 36 years of teaching, you are the worst child I've ever had!" I felt honored.

When I went into the fifth grade, they gave us IQ tests. I wanted to get out of there and go play, so I just went down the sheet and checked all the answers randomly. After all, I was supposed to be "dumb," right? My teacher, Mrs. Linebaugh, called my mother and told her I was "severely retarded" and needed to be put back at least two grades.

My mother told her I was faking, and then spanked me again.

Mrs. Linebaugh took another look at me. She had been a "tomboy" herself, and had spent her childhood playing wild Indian in the swamps of Florida with her brothers and their pet raccoon. I think she sensed a kindred spirit. She started reading books to the class every day. Not the icky dumb Dick and Jane junk all the other teachers made us read, but a book about a pair of sisters during World War II who smuggled English pilots out of Paris with the underground. She read us the *Diary of Anne Frank*. All of a sudden, I really wanted to read. If you could read stories like these, maybe reading wasn't such a drag after all. Maybe it was worth the effort. Mrs. Linebaugh began giving me stuff to read—good stuff! Stuff I wanted to read. It got so all I wanted to do was read. I read *Little Men, The Secret Garden, Little Women,* a book of Greek legends that a friend of my mother's gave me. I read *Grimm's Fairy Tales* and *Aesop's Fables* and Laura Ingalls Wilder's *Little House* series. I read *Penrod,* about another adventurous child who was always in trouble. At the end of the year Mrs. Linebaugh gave us another IQ test. This time she told me to really try and not just check off anything, but to really read the questions and do my best. By then I loved her so much I really wanted to do well. I tested at the 11th-grade level in reading. She said "I thought so!" and smiled at me.

Years later, after going back to the University of New Mexico in my forties to finally get my college degree and go on to get a master's degree in counseling, I was searching for a practicum. I'd been a working artist for most of my adult life, and wanted to use art in my counseling work. A new program was just beginning through the college, and they were looking for people to help develop and implement it. It would use art and counseling to help children at risk in the poorest neighborhoods in Albuquerque. My old neighborhood where Emerson Elementary School was located was now known as "The War Zone" because of the prevalence of crime and violence. The program asked me to go back to Emerson.

Just walking through the halls was frightening for me. I remembered the pain and humiliation I had suffered there.

It looked different—so much smaller. I remembered I was bigger. The place was the same. But Mrs. Martin wasn't there anymore. She had been replaced by a wonderful warm and kind woman, Mrs. Gonzales. I thought of Richard. Now, they taught all the children Spanish and celebrated their differences! Mrs. Gonzales welcomed me into that old awful office I knew so well, but she was anxious to hear my ideas and point of view. She told me that there were children in the school who spoke 17 different languages. She wanted them all to feel welcome, not only to their school, but also to the United States, their new country. She said she was so happy to have me there to help the children. It was one of the best days of my life.

I went on to use my art and counseling skills to work with some really amazing children. For those who were lonely and missing their old homes in Mexico, Viet Nam and Cuba we used art to express that loneliness. We made pictures for fathers who were in prison. We talked about how hard it is to learn sometimes, when other things are crowding your life. But the best part was that these kids were learning. They were learning to read, and to think and to feel. They were learning a new language, English, and how to express themselves in that language. Nobody got spanked for speaking Spanish anymore. I was home. I was doing good work.

BASE BRATS: ALBUQUERQUE, 1956

There were a hundred kids within a block, endless days of roller-skating, bike rides, hide-and-seek. Most of the kids were "Base Brats" in that neighborhood bordered by Kirtland Air Force Base, Sandia Laboratories, and Manzano Base. Every kid heard words at home like *nuclear, plutonium, Q-clearance, radioactive, Geiger counter, half-life, uranium, megaton, mushroom-cloud,* and heard of places named White Sands, Nevada, Eniwetok, Hiroshima, Nagasaki. Kids had lived in all fifty states, and countries all over the globe.

We knew we were a Russian target, might be vaporized like the people in Nagasaki, turned into a photograph. Newer bombs were hundreds of times more powerful. The world's largest stockpile, inside Manzano Mountain, was five miles away.

We couldn't talk outside the family. There were stories: they could make your dad disappear. There were kids whose dads had disappeared. In a flurry of quick grief, the family was "transferred." We never really knew what happened, but we were scared.

Any weekday morning the Base roared. We sat obediently in our desks, trying to concentrate on math problems, spelling lists. Like we didn't notice the rattling windowpanes, the rumble through our bodies. We looked out the window for a billowing mushroom-cloud, flying gray ash, but all was clear blue sky. Our teacher blithely continued drilling us on our multiplication tables.

Dads were often "stationed" elsewhere. My best friend Carol's dad was on Eniwetok. She was born in Japan, and her little brother, Billy, in Germany. Her sister Laurie was born here, in Albuquerque. We argued about whether Billy could be President, since he was born in a foreign country. Carol said he could because he was born on base, and that was the same as being born in the US. I wasn't so sure. Laurie was four and had little blonde braids. Carol was jealous. She had thick, curly brown hair like her mother's, always a wild tangled mess.

Carol couldn't stop talking about her dad coming home. Laurie couldn't remember him, but she and Billy pretended they did when Carol talked about him. Carol's mom made Kool-Aid for all the kids, and always let us come and play at their house. Carol's grandpa looked just like Fred Mertz on *I Love Lucy*. But her grandma didn't look like Ethel. She looked like a little-old-lady version of Laurie.

Finally, their dad came home, but only to the base. Carol was angry and sad. They had to run tests on him. He couldn't come home until his radiation levels went down. Her mom explained it wouldn't be safe for the family, especially her, sleeping next to him in the same bed. Carol suggested he could sleep on the couch, but her mom said no. They had to wait thirty days, until he was "cleared."

Years later, I heard Carol's dad had died of leukemia at forty-two. I remembered him, so big, so strong, a soldier in his uniform: her father, through Carol's eyes, when we were nine.

1953-54

Andrew Paquet, Jr.

Apricots and Tortillas

In 1945 my parents thought their family was complete. They had two daughters, one fourteen and the other five. Then came the surprise—me. My parents, being true to their generation, had always wanted a son, and there I was. They were delighted. At least my parents were, I'm not so sure how my sisters felt.

I was an easy birth, and pushed my way into the world with a full head of hair and dimples. They thought I was perfect. But then the doctor told them about my heart. I had been born with a serious heart murmur.

My parents had been through the Depression of the 1930s and a World War, so they were used to challenges. And because my father was a Methodist minister they accepted my condition as the will of God, perhaps. They only mentioned it in cautioning me against running too hard and exempting me from physical education class in school.

We moved to Albuquerque in 1955 when I was ten. Life was good for me. My only worry was learning how to spell "Albuquerque."

It may have been that my parents worried about my health but discussed it only in Spanish. I was growing up in two different worlds. My parents' families were from Mexico and Spain. They spoke Spanish to each other, but taught me only English. It was a time in our country that many Hispanic people felt discriminated against and changed their names, and did not teach their children Spanish. There was a smoky wisp of prejudice still present, even in Albuquerque.

We lived in an Anglo neighborhood in the Northeast Heights. We had a simple three- bedroom home. It had a nice yard with flowers, shade trees and one apricot tree in the backyard. My parents gave me the job of picking all the ripe apricots before the birds got them. I didn't really like the job, but I loved apricots.

Our neighborhood may have been Anglo but our kitchen was straight from Mexico. My mother would bake apricot empanadas and have them ready when I came home from school. If apricots weren't in season, I could count on coming home to fresh warm flour tortillas with butter.

The only worry about my health that parents expressed in English was about my size and whether I was growing. I was small and skinny. They purchased vitamins and nutritional supplements in hopes I would grow. Those were also the days of home milk delivery. Our milkman was short but apparently of acceptable height. Our refrigerator was about five feet tall, and my mother hoped I would be at least as tall as the refrigerator or the milkman. That sounded funny to me, hoping I would at least be as tall as the milkman.

I am now the tallest in our family at 5 feet 10 inches. My parents only needed to wait for my late-adolescent growth spurt in high school. Later, when I was looking at some old family photos with my father when he was in his 80s, he commented, "I wonder what we were feeding you to make you grow?" I told him, "Apricots and tortillas."

I wonder if without the unique blend of our Anglo neighborhood apricot tree and my mother's tortillas from Mexico I would be the me who I am today. I mean much more than just my height.

What was true of me in the 1950's was true of Albuquerque. It was a city that represented diversity. It had multiple languages, types of people and different religions. It was a military town, it was a university town, it was an old historic town, and it was a leading edge, scientific, atomic age new town. It was a western cowboy, Native American, ranching, oil and gas town. It was a railroad town. It was a fantastic place to grow up.

The Invisible Methodist

My parents were very involved in the Spanish Methodist Church. My father was a lay minister and served as a pastor in several small mission churches in Santa Fe and Albuquerque. I sat through long church services, but because I understood hardly a word, I would daydream. For instance:

Can everyone see me okay? Are you sure? You think you can, but I'm really invisible!

What would you do if you *were* invisible? Haven't we all pondered this question? When I was growing up there was a television show called *The Invisible Man*. The "Invisible Man" was a scientist who solved crimes. Through a lab mishap he became permanently invisible. To interact with the public, he wrapped himself in gauze tape, like a mummy; and wore a suit, hat and sunglasses. When he wanted to be invisible, he simply unwrapped his outfit.

The show made me curious about some aspects of invisibility. If you could turn it on and off at will, that would be magical. If you didn't want to be called on in class, you could become invisible (after roll was taken). You would hear the teacher saying; "Has anybody seen Andy? He was just here."

The advantages of being invisible were obvious to me or any other child who liked to pay pranks. You could play tricks on your friends and family. But there probably were some problems with being invisible. For example, would those automatic doors work for you? Could you play sports? "Throw me the ball, I'm clear."

As the service droned on, my mind would wander and I thought about things I could do if I were invisible. But, no matter how much I really, really thought about sneaking into the girls' locker room, as a Methodist, I knew there were certain boundaries, "invisible boundaries," that I shouldn't cross.

Nevertheless, as an invisible Methodist, I could still have fun and play tricks.

In church, I could sneak up to the altar and blow out the candles. I could turn the sheet music pages as the organist was trying to play. Best of all, I would not have to put my comic book money in the collection plates, but that might be sinful, and so perhaps I would sneak some coins into the offering plates as it passed by. Would the other worshipers wonder how these visible coins floated into the plates? A miracle, they would imagine. Remember those times when somebody dropped the offering plate? Think: invisible Methodist prankster.

Oh, it would be hard being an invisible Methodist!

A Methodist Kid at Hanukkah

As a young boy, my knowledge of religion was simply that I went to church, where there were pews and ministers and Bibles. I also thought vacation Bible school was fun, mainly for the craft projects. Some aunts and uncles were Catholic, so I had heard of priests and going to Mass.

The first Jewish person I ever knew was my fifth-grade friend Bobby, who lived down the street. His family's religion was not a noticeable thing to me. I had friends who went to many different churches. It wasn't a big issue in the mind of a fifth-grader, not as important as playing marbles, riding a bike or a developing interest in girls. I didn't even know words like "synagogue" or "temple." Maybe I had heard a rabbi mentioned, but certainly the term "circumcision" wasn't in my vocabulary. All I did know was that at Christmas time Jewish families decorated for Hanukkah and had those candle things. I thought it was neat to get presents every night for eight days. Maybe I was aware that Bobby had to learn some Hebrew.

Once I was invited to their house for dinner during Hanukkah. I was scared. I didn't know what to expect or how to act, or what was proper and what wasn't. I was afraid I would do or say the wrong thing. There were some rudimentary facts running through my mind. I knew Jewish families did not eat certain foods. In those days, I knew Catholic families ate fish on Fridays but I didn't know why. I thought I had heard that special china was used only during Hanukkah and not on other regular days. I was so nervous that I would do something stupid and offend my friend's family. I didn't know what to eat or not to eat. Was it okay to drink milk? What if I slipped up and mentioned Jesus? I didn't know whether I did anything wrong or not. If I did, they certainly didn't point it out to me, but maybe they had a good laugh later.

Bobby's relatives owned Magison's Restaurant downtown, which was one of my favorite places to eat. Bobby even had a birthday party there one time, which was so neat. Later, when I was older, I would occasionally meet my father for lunch at Magison's, so it had good memories.

A Bilingual Bicycle Mystery
(with subtitles)

When I was a child my parents spoke Spanish, unless they were talking to me, in which case they spoke English. The language I spoke, understood, read and wrote was English. But somewhere in my brain I stored a drawer full of miscellaneous Spanish. The following story is based on my adventures, some real and some imaginary, as a result of having a drawer full of Spanish.

I wake up by the side of the road, lying next to a bicycle. I don't remember how I got there or who I am. I have no identification. I don't even have the dime in the bottom of my shoe I usually carried for Cub Scout dues.

After checking myself for injuries, I find I am able to get back on the bicycle. I assume it is mine, but I don't know what direction I was going. Since I am on the east side of the road, I head north slowly to see if something jars my memory. I come to a residential area and stop at the first house to ask if they will call the police for help. A woman answers the door and says, "Hola, Andres, que tal?" (*Hello, Andrew, how are you?*) I don't remember if I speak Spanish or not but I say "Ayudame, por favor" and muchas mas palabras *("Help me" and many more words)*; but I don't understand what I am saying. "Ay Dios Mio!"*(OMG)* It's as if I am speaking in tongues, hablando en lenguas. The woman laughs. I guess I am funny in Spanish or maybe she is laughing at my adventure clothing, Lone Ranger Tee Shirt, and Davy Crockett hat.

"Ven *(Come,)*" she motions me to come in. I am puzzled, is my name Ben or Andres? I am trying to clear my mind and remember who I am. As I enter the house, I see the walls are filled with pictures of family. I pass a mirror on the wall, and see a cute young boy who is bleeding from a scratch on his face. I've seen him before. He is in several of the pictures. Por amor de Dios *(OMG)*, it's me!

This is getting confusing, my mind is starting to swirl and I feel faint. Just then an elderly man enters the room and says "Don Andres *(Mr. Andrew)*, I am not going to undress." Why is he saying that. Is he crazy?

From a corner run several children and a big black, curly dog that knocks me down. I hit my head and black out for a second. My face is being rapidly washed; no, it's the dog licking my face. I am wet with slobber, but actually comforted by his efforts. The woman says in English, "Andy, your dog is happy to see you." I recognize her. She's my mother. Oh my gosh, my memory is back! Bumping my head again must have brought it all back. The dog saved the day. It just goes to show "El perro es el mejor amigo del hombre" *("The dog is man's best friend")*.

AUTHOR BIOGRAPHIES

Lynn Ewing (maiden name Flora)

I was born in Albuquerque at Presbyterian Hospital nine months after my father's return from duty during the Korean War. My parents took me home to join my older brother in the adobe house they had built themselves, even making their own adobes. A year later, my younger brother was born. When I was six we moved into another adobe house, this one designed by my parents but built by a professional.

I was too much a daydreamer to be a good student, but I loved to read. When I was nine I was introduced to Nancy Drew mysteries and to Louisa May Alcott's books. I was so enthralled with Nancy Drew that I began sneaking out my window at night to go solve "mysteries" I made up. I loved riding bikes, climbing trees, swimming and helping in the garden.

María Leyba

I was born and raised in the barrio of Barelas, where I still reside in my family home with my husband and pets. Barelas is only eight blocks south of downtown Albuquerque, but in the 1950's we had no paved streets, sidewalks, or indoor toilets. In my home only Spanish was spoken. As I gradually learned English I also began to teach my mother my new language. Even as a young child I became my mother's interpreter and her eyes. As a Mexican albino, mama had limited vision, so it was my job to help her navigate around our community. When I was ten I discovered the public library on Edith and Central. In the summers I walked every day to the library just to smell the books and bring some of them home with me.

I loved public speaking and reciting poetry. My favorite activity was performing in community plays at the Barelas Community Center and at Coronado Elementary. Despite living in a barrio I was the happiest little girl growing up, discovering my world.

Lisa Myers

I grew up in the Albuquerque's Northeast Heights. My father, Phil Eakins, was the sportscaster for KOB television. He died when I was two years old, which of course changed my life irrevocably.

I attended Yucca Elementary School. While I was a good student, I didn't much enjoy going to school because all those rules cramped my style. I lived two blocks from the "A Pool" and I spent almost all summer there. Swimming is by far my fondest childhood memory. Roller-skating was something else I totally loved. I had a regular route mapped out, so I knew where the dangerous cracks in the sidewalk were, as well as the houses where they might yell at me if I went on their circular driveway.

I rode my bike to the Hoffmantown Library every Saturday. I returned the two books I had checked out the week before and spent a long time browsing for the two I would check out this time. If I were very lucky, my mother would give me a dollar, and I could look around to my heart's content at Ben Franklin's. No matter what else I purchased, I always got a square cinnamon sucker. Every single Monday evening my mother took my three sisters and me to Furr's Cafeteria.

Andrew Paquet Jr. ("Sonny")

I was the last of three children and only son, hence the "Jr." and nickname "Sonny," but I was really just "Andy," even though when the phone rang, we had to discern whether the caller wanted "big Andy" or "little Andy." I grew up among friends near the Highland Theater, where for a dime you could catch the shows on Saturday and sneak in candy from Woolworth's next door. I liked the tiny wax bottle-shaped candy with juice inside that you got to by biting off the wax top.

I went to Zia Elementary, Jefferson Junior High and Highland High School. I was small and somewhat shy, but developed a sense of humor to get some attention. My friends were from the nearest houses to ours; we all went to the same Methodist church, were in Boy Scouts and Methodist Youth Fellowship together. I was taught to be good, to follow the "Golden Rule" and most of all, with an occasional shaking of my shoulders to remind me, "to use my head." This last directive also came also because, with my heart condition, my parents knew I could not get a job doing manual labor. It was a good directive, as I became a scientist as a result of my amazement at the wonders of nature, some of which occurred on camping trips with the Boy Scouts. I had a wonderful career as a microbiology professor.

Susan Paquet (maiden name Smith)

I grew up in the 1950's in Albuquerque. We lived in a neighborhood near Louisiana and Central (Route 66), a section of town now known as "The War Zone" because of the rival gang activities. "The War Zone" was perhaps, even in the Fifties, an appropriate name for the area, as it was squeezed between Kirtland Military Base and Sandia Military Base.

My neighborhood was one of tract Pueblo style homes. The houses were built on straight lined streets with each house looking exactly the same, except for the color of stucco chosen by the family. It was a neighborhood of military families, Hispanic families, a few Native American families and the category known as other. That was me, the "other," a daughter of an Anglo plumbing contractor. I spent most of my childhood just trying to find myself a place to belong.

Georgia Santa Maria

I was born in the big purple brick hospital, then St. Joseph's, now on Martin Luther King (then on Grande), to two alcoholic frat kids among the general whoopee atmosphere following WWII. As a kid, my mom used to "farm me out" to various friends and relatives on the weekends so she could enjoy her life—but the great thing was she had fabulous taste in friends and relatives. Most of them loved me and took wonderful care of me. I had a terrific ecumenical childhood with lots of adventure. Eddie introduced me to AA at his kitchen table, where early meetings were held in the 50's, and I learned the Twelve Steps. Also, poker and fishing, his other favorite things. My grandmothers taught me to cook and sew, and gave me fabulous books and dollies to sew for. Bobby taught me the names of all the plants, everything about the Sandias, and gave me a love of history and politics. Frieda taught me how to be a sick kid the year I had mono, and gave me wonderful art supplies, the Greek myths, and Jewish spirituality. Hebi took me into her tribe of kids; I joined them in numerous outings and adventures, including "Ban the Bomb" rallies. Concha was my Fairy Godmother who taught me about womanpower, Spanish history, ballet and flamenco. My uncle Wally taught me about growing up in New Zealand, and read to me in his fabulous British accent. Matt was a scientist-astronomer, and taught me why stars twinkle. Sam loved classical music, and taught me how to think up great stories while listening. Grandad was friends with all of the original Taos artists, and took me with him to visit them and see their art. Gilbert, Pilar, Steffi, Clara and Albert invited us to the dances, and taught me about Pueblo life. Grandpa was a marvelous storyteller, a former friend of gangsters in Capone's Chicago and a WWII spy. He was larger than life, and mad about me. Eve Younghunter taught me how to make proper English Tea, in a proper English teapot, and how to dance the tango to her wind-up Victrola.

In school, I was always in trouble; non-conformity just came naturally to me. I thought school was dull and dumb and generally a waste of my time. But I was always up for punching the kid who teased the homely girl or the poor kid in ragged clothes, right square in the mouth. Preferably with a roller-skate in my hand, so as not to bang-up my knuckles. Grandpa taught me that.

Cynthia Sylvester

I was born in Albuquerque, New Mexico, to the *Kiyaa'anni* (Towering House) Clan for the *Bilagaana* (White) Clan. We were a bi-racial family long before any of us knew what that was and how it might shape our lives. Growing up in New Mexico it really was no big deal and I always say, "My brother and sister and I just thought we were Protestants with a really good tan." We lived out in what we called the country, but now they call the suburbs and the stories that I write are really a reflection of being this little band of Indians, my mom and dad's band, off the reservation.

I wrote "Legend of the High Noon Moon" as a response to wanting to have an Indian legend to tell. "Two Crows Laughing" is my response to how my family deals with the little and the big tragedies that face us at any age—to laugh.

www.ingramcontent.com/pod-product-compliance
Lightning Source LLC
Chambersburg PA
CBHW021222260626
47172CB00002B/553